Moments Parfaits
in Paris

Text and Photography by Sylvaine Lang
Published by Moments Parfaits

Moments Parfaits in Paris

ISBN: 978-0-9993849-0-9

Graphic design by Raegan Roche

Printed by The Parks Group
Modesto, California

First edition published in November 2017 by Moments Parfaits
www.momentsparfaits.com

for my father

*The real voyage of discovery
consists not in seeking new landscapes,
but in having new eyes.*

Marcel Proust

Contents

Preface

I hold my father responsible for triggering my love affair with America. I was merely six years old when he spent four months in Arizona and delighted us with his tales of the Grand Canyon, the Painted Desert, and the Petrified Forest: the actual settings of the Western movies we watched on our black and white TV set every Sunday afternoon. I had just turned nineteen when he drove me to the airport: I eagerly caught a plane to spend the summer in California and travel across the United States. At twenty-four, I married a handsome American I had met during my very first trip and moved to Modesto with two suitcases, one filled with clothes, the other with books.

Being away from my native land made me aware of the many things I had taken for granted. At that time, leeks and Belgian endives were conspicuously absent from the produce section and cheese was packaged in bricks of two colors: yellow or white. If I wanted a croissant for breakfast, I had to make my own, from scratch. One Christmas, I talked to four different butchers before finding one who could help me in my quest for a Guinea hen; the other three had never heard of this delicious bird. On the other hand, my life was filled with new foods, new places, new people, and the ongoing discovery of a new culture.

Many expatriates will tell you they are ambivalent about calling any place "home:" after a while, they feel they don't really belong anywhere. Thanks to unconventional career choices –at least by French standards– my personal experience has been different: I truly have two homes and two cultures. My numerous, lengthy trips back to France allowed me to keep one foot in each country. And yet, the physical and emotional distance also altered the way I look at the country of my youth. I've been granted a new pair of eyes and a new mindset. This dual perspective has challenged my travel habits. I still enjoy my old haunts but I also devised a fun game to explore a random area of Paris on every trip; it is a little bit like throwing darts at a map. It has taken me to pockets of the city I had never visited before and I discover them with the fresh eyes of a first-time visitor. The way I document my travel in photographs has morphed: whether I'm shooting a familiar place or a new scene, I try to capture a feeling, a moment.

Five years ago, my father was diagnosed with ALS. As the implacable illness was robbing him of his motor functions, his mind and sense of humor remained as sharp as ever. He was a gifted storyteller and we spent countless days reminiscing about his parents, his youth, and my own childhood. We shared some good laughs and a few tears. The journey back in time and the exchange of memories prompted me to revisit some specific locations in Paris that we had discussed. I wanted to see how much they had changed. I found that places truly come to life when they are infused with meaning: our narratives transcend their intrinsic beauty or banality.

Paris has been a constant source of inspiration for writers and photographers. Here it serves as the backdrop for some of my favorite stories. This book is a presentation of "my" Paris where I introduce you to forty locations throughout the city: some will strike you as familiar, others are more obscure. All of them are paired with a personal anecdote and strive to show that even a monumental city like Paris can –and should– be approached on a small scale. It is an invitation for every visitor to challenge the bucket list dogma and (re)discover the capital from a personal point of view. It is an ode to the little things, the touching details, and the funny situations that make each life unique. It is an encouragement to build your very own collection of *Moments Parfaits* and to share them with the people you love.

Sylvaine Lang
Modesto, August 2017

Merci!

Heartfelt thanks go to Raegan Roche for helping me bring my ideas into focus when I was still wrestling with the very concept of the book. Throughout this project, you have been my unwavering fan, providing thoughtful encouragement when I doubted myself and challenging me to produce the best writing I could. I am forever grateful for the countless hours you spent designing this book and bringing my photography to life on the page.

I also want to thank Andria Resendes not just because you are an eagle-eyed proofreader but also for inspiring me to become a better photographer: your uncanny ability to pick out details and your sense of aesthetics have forced me to consider locations, scenery, and life situations in general with a new set of eyes.

Finally, this book would not exist without the contributions of my whole family (and a few close friends) who unwittingly gave me so much material to weave into my stories; and without my husband Rick: thank you for your patience and support while I spent long hours on the computer, and for being my faithful traveling companion in life and in flights across the ocean. Your deep love of France is *la cerise sur le gâteau*.

Moments Parfaits

in Paris

Silver scissors

Her fate was sealed. Her boss had told her *"Vous avez un avenir dans la vente, Mademoiselle."* A future in sales. It was my mother's first job, a sales clerk at Les Ciseaux d'Argent on rue de Rivoli. In the late Fifties, this shop sold very elegant men's wear. Mom had a knack for merchandising: without the benefit of any marketing class, she instinctively knew how to upsell and accessorize by suggesting the perfect tie or *pochette* to complement the suit and shirt the customer had already selected. Her sales career was derailed when I was born: more than anything else, Mom wanted to be a mom. While my sister and I were growing up, she still did holiday stints –Christmas, Mother's Day– at a couple of shops that would have hired her back full time in a heartbeat. But her heart was somewhere else.

Mom and I walked by Les Ciseaux d'Argent a few years ago. The old, fond memories bubbled up but I could tell she had no regrets: she still owns up to her choices and is happy with them. I revisited that spot recently and was saddened to see that "her" shop had been taken over by a cheap souvenir emporium: mini Eiffel towers, Sacré-Coeur snow globes, and I Heart Paris T-shirts had replaced woolens, silks, and cashmere. I did not have the heart to tell Mom. Of course, the rue de Rivoli arcades still house lovely institutions like Angelina and Le Meurice, where Salvador Dali was a regular. One of the longest streets in Paris, it stretches from église Saint Paul (3rd arr.) to place de la Concorde (8th arr.) and lines the Louvre and the Tuileries Gardens.

Les Ciseaux d'Argent
156 rue de Rivoli, 1st arr.

Rouge

I'm told that women like heels. High heels. In Sex and the City, Carrie Bradshaw probably did more for stilettos than all of Madison Avenue advertising execs combined. Strangely, I've never lusted after shoes; I blame it on my long, skinny feet. Shopping for shoes for me is akin to a trip to the dentist for others, save for the insurance reimbursement. Then, there is Andria who showed up for her job interview in 4" heels. For a warehouse position. I suggested she might consider a change of footwear when she got the job and she scoffed: flats were uncomfortable to her. I thought of her when I stood in front of Christian Louboutin's *atelier* in Galerie Véro-Dodat. A thirtyish Parisienne strolled as I was framing my shot: the long blond hair, the tailored black coat, the red skirt, the red purse, the red heels… Were the soles red too? I believe they were. She paced back and forth, intently looking at the window display. She moved on. She came back. She paced some more. She left again. Maybe she didn't need another pair of red heels. Maybe she came back later.

Galerie Véro-Dodat is one of the passages couverts that dot the central area of Paris between the Grands Boulevards and the Louvre. Built in the early 19th century, the passages were the ancestors to our indoor shopping malls: their glass roofs offered rain protection and the tiled floors were a vast improvement over the Paris muddy streets, especially for high-class ladies wearing fancy footwear. Vero-Dodat was opened by two charcutiers (yes, pork butchers) and links rue Jean-Jacques Rousseau and rue Croix-des-Petits-Champs. The shops arched windows are all identical, dark wood with copper and iron trim, mirrors, paintings, and columns.

Galerie Véro-Dodat
Between rue Jean-Jacques Rousseau and rue Croix-des-Petits-Champs, 1st arr.

This little piggy went to market

Raegan and I had just settled into our rented studio near Place des Victoires. It was close to 3 pm and she was hungry: the croissant and fruit cup that were offered for breakfast on the plane had served their initial purpose but additional fuel would be needed to wander around the city. I suggested we walked to rue Coquillière: bordering Les Halles, the old wholesale food market, I was sure we would find an open restaurant there. We grabbed an outside table at Au Pied de Cochon and ordered their famous *soupe à l'oignon*, topped with loads of crusty bread and gooey cheese. We finished off with an espresso. Instead of a mundane chocolate square, it was served with the cutest pink meringue, shaped like the head of a pig. Smart. Sweet. Smiles.

I read Emile Zola's Le Ventre de Paris after Les Halles were relocated to Rungis. I'm surely romanticizing the experience but I would have liked to walk around Guimard's elegant steel and glass pavilions, gathering rounds of aged goat cheese and a poulet de Bresse for dinner. Forum des Halles, the shopping center built on the site of the food market in the Seventies did not age very well; new architecture, gardens, and shops made a grand appearance in 2016. In the meantime, some of the restaurants that fed the butchers, greengrocers, and fishmongers of yesteryears are still lining the rue Coquillère, including Au Pied de Cochon which has been open every hour of every day since 1947. Check out the gilded pig feet on your way to the restroom.

Au Pied de Cochon
6 rue Coquillère, 1st arr.

Slow Food

Mom's side of the family is rooted in the Charentes. My grandparents were born in Angoulême and eventually retired in Royan, on the Atlantic coast. Pépé René was extremely meticulous and his vegetable garden looked like a very organized army: rows of carrots, leeks, and radishes, all perfectly aligned and of matching heights; straight, narrow footpaths of packed dirt separating the slightly raised beds; pristine galvanized watering cans and glistening tools without a spec of rust on them. He grew the most succulent tomatoes and I would sneak out in the garden before breakfast to eat some of the bite-size fruits: they tasted like candy. But there was another kind of treasure in his backyard, one that could not yield to his will or his care. Two sides of the property were lined with a hedge of privets and they were home to *cagouilles*! Short of going to the nearby beaches, my favorite activity in Royan was to hunt for snails with pépé. He would fetch a large bucket and we would dutifully inspect every shrub of the hedge, plucking every *petit-gris* snail in sight. See, the Charentais love snails so much that they even coined a regional word: while everybody else refers to them as *escargots*, the Charentais call them *cagouilles*. The *petit-gris* species was plentiful then and reputed to have an even more delicate taste than its larger cousin, the *escargot de Bourgogne*. After a successful hunt, we would trust the gastropods to grandma's expert care. And a few days later, the heady smell of garlic butter filled the kitchen.

Due to its proximity to Les Halles, rue Montorgueil has been a food lover's paradise for centuries. Many of the shops, cafés, and restaurants have become institutions such as L'Escargot Montorgueil. With its splendid architecture, a jet black rough iron façade with gold accents, and a sumptuous spiral staircase, it truly deserves to be designated a monument historique. Fear not: the menu is quite comprehensive but, of course, snails are the specialty of the house and have been served at this location since 1832.

L'Escargot Montorgeuil
38 rue Montorgueil, 2nd arr.

Un franc les trois citrons

If you grew up in France in the early Sixties, there was no escaping the *marché* experience. Supermarkets were nonexistent but bi-weekly open-air markets meant that fresh edibles were brought to just about every town from Les Halles. On Saturday mornings, Mom would head out to the *place du marché* in Vitry-sur-Seine with little Sylvaine in tow. Mom did not drive but the marché was only three hundred yards from the apartment where we lived. As a six-year old girl, my eyes were just about level with the stalls brimming with stacks of large brown eggs, butter mountains to be cut *à la motte*, dressed rabbits with their fuzzy feet still attached, glistening fish waiting to be expertly filleted, and perfect rows of fruits and vegetables that no one dared to touch. The aisles were noisy and bustling with anxious shoppers; I knew not to let go of Mom's hand for fear of getting carried away by the crowd. One day, as I lowered my sight, a gnarly weathered hand holding three lemons appeared. I heard a tiny fraying voice whispering *"Un franc les trois citrons; un franc les trois citrons."* It sounded more like a plea than a sales call. The old lady with a dowager's hump seemed frail and tired. Dressed in black and gray, she was pulling an old-fashioned market stroller from which she would occasionally extract a triplet of plump yellow fruits, the only thing she had to sell. I looked up; our eyes met; she moved on. The brief encounter left me with so many puzzling questions: why was she working at her age? Didn't she have a family to take care of her? What if she had been my grandma? Where did she live? Was there a lemon tree in her garden? How many lemons did she sell? From that point on, I looked for her every Saturday. I saw her every Saturday until we moved. I never exchanged a word with her. Fifty years later, I still wonder about her life story.

Strolling the markets is one of my favorite activities. Part of the appeal is that each one has its own personality. You could argue that tomatoes and leeks look the same everywhere but the shoppers, the sellers, and the ambiance greatly differ with the location. From fashionable Mouffetard and Raspail to ebullient Barbès and Belleville, visiting the neighborhood markets gives you a unique insight into the locals.

Evening before market day, in front of La Bourse
Palais Brongniart, 2nd arr.

Little Egypt

Truth be told, I was not enamored with history when I was growing up. It just felt like a futile exercise in memorizing dates and battles: 1515 Marignan! 1815 Waterloo! Things changed dramatically when Madame Alfroi became my history-geography professor in *Sixième*. I was eleven years old and this remarkable woman made such an impression on me that her teachings still resonate loudly. With her black rimmed cat eye glasses and her auburn hair in a tight bun, she looked like the proverbial librarian. The syllabus focused on ancient civilizations: Egypt, Mesopotamia, Greece, Rome… The novelty of the subjects paired with her uncanny talent for (his)storytelling made her class the most exciting one of the year. I was mesmerized. I dreamed of pyramids, papyrus, and pharaohs. In June 1969, she took the whole class to the Antiquities department of Le Louvre so we could contemplate a real mummy. *Incroyable!* To this day, I still think of Madame Alfroi whenever I lay my eyes on something Egyptian.

I was not the only French to be fascinated by ancient Egypt. Following Bonaparte's epic Egyptian Campaign (1798-1801, if you like to memorize dates) and Champollion's decoding of hieroglyphic script, it seems that all of Paris was swept off by Egyptomania. The Luxor Obelisk on place de la Concorde is the best-known example but Egyptian architectural elements can be found all over the city: tombs at the Père-Lachaise cemetery, fountains on place du Châtelet and rue de Sèvres, the porch of the Hôtel de Beauharnais… Parts of Le Sentier literally transport you to Little Egypt; just follow rue d'Aboukir, rue du Nil, or rue d'Alexandrie to Place du Caire and three effigies of the cow Goddess Hathor will usher you into the Passage du Caire.

Passage du Caire
Between place du Caire and rue St-Denis, 2nd arr.

Steampunk

I was about eight years old when I first set foot in the métro. I was intrigued by the uniformed man who punched holes in our tickets before allowing us onto the platform; I imagined the confetti accumulating at his feet gave a festive touch to an otherwise dull job. Eventually, the tunnels of beveled white ceramic tiles and the enamel signage became a familiar sight. Discovering the Louvre station after its complete remodel in the late Sixties was a marvelous revelation: the classic color scheme had given way to a décor reminiscent of the museum itself, complete with mood lighting and stone alcoves sheltering replica statues and artworks. More recently, the Arts et Métiers station on *Ligne 11* benefited from a similar cultural makeover. I felt immediately transported to the Nautilus of 20,000 Leagues Under the Sea: copper-clad walls, brass accents, huge wheels and gears hanging out from the ceiling, and shadow boxes shaped like portholes displaying models of inventions featured in the museum "on the surface." The only thing missing was a giant octopus lurking in the dark tunnel.

Musée des Arts et Métiers celebrates human ingenuity. As a repository of scientific and technical knowledge, its vast collection includes inventions dating back to the 15th century: Pascal's mechanical calculator, A. Graham Bell's telephone, Bartholdi's original model for the Statue of Liberty, the Lumière brothers' cinematograph… Monumental objects such as Foucault's pendulum and the plane flown by Blériot across the English Channel are displayed inside the 12th-century church of Saint-Martin-des Champs.

Musée des Arts et Métiers
60 rue Réaumur, 3rd arr.

Rain on my parade

I own one raincoat: a classic tailored green gabardine that my aunt Maguy made for me in the late Seventies. Although it still fits, it permanently resides in a dark corner of the hall closet. Indispensable when I lived in France, it became superfluous as soon as I moved to the Central Valley of California. It is now a beloved relic of times past. As a little girl, my French wardrobe always included a pair of rubber boots and a shiny slicker with a matching hat. I then became the nerdy kid who carried a plastic rain bonnet in her coat pocket: who doesn't remember those dreadful transparent squares that folded like an accordion? I thus acquired the ability to restore an unfurled Michelin road map to its original pristine state, a skill that altogether denotes another kind of nerdiness. Eventually, I ditched practicality for style and an automatic umbrella found a home in my school bag. I really should know better but I often forget to bring rain gear when I travel to France. I have purchased several 5 or 10-euro umbrellas from the "entrepreneurs" who conveniently appear as you exit the métro on a rainy day: these cheap *parapluies* barely stand up to a sudden gust of wind, rarely outlast a steady downpour, and usually find themselves quickly discarded into a street *poubelle*. Maybe it is time for me to invest in an elegant full-size umbrella, preferably adorned with distinctive carvings on the handle: something that could double up as a chic walking stick when the need occurs. Especially when I know exactly where to take it for repair if the need occurs. I am still a practical girl after all…

Umbrella repair is a lost art: only two craftsmen in France will restore your umbrella to its former splendor and usefulness. Thierry Millet recycles thousands of parts and officiates as the umbrella doctor at Maison Pep's in the Passage de l'Ancre. This uncovered alleyway is considered to be the oldest in Paris. Hidden behind tall blue doors on Rue Saint-Martin, the narrow passage is lined with colorful façades and workshops, pots are filled with luscious plants and flowers, walls sport old-fashioned lamps and unique signage (don't miss the siren). Mainly residential, it is rarely accessible during weekends and closes at 6 pm on weekdays. Definitely worth a stroll, even if you don't use umbrellas.

Passage de l'Ancre
Between rue de Turbigo and rue Saint-Martin, 3rd Arr.

Budding photographer

Santa Claus had been good to me. He brought me a camera. My very first camera. It was a boxy Agfa-Gevaert model housed in a dark brown leather case. There was also one tall skinny roll of film. I was seven and ecstatic. The following Sunday, I begged Dad to take me somewhere –anywhere– to shoot that first roll. Of course, he obliged. We usually went to the Bois de Vincennes on Sundays, often with the strap-on roller skates, sometimes with my fat tire bike: I would loop around the *vélodrome* and he would jog by my side. This time, we headed out to the zoo. It was not my first visit but, this time, I had the means to document the outing. He carefully loaded the roll for me and let me snap pictures blissfully. When that roll was processed, it revealed twenty-four black and white images of truncated giraffes, blurry elephants, and vertical stripes that presumably belonged to a couple of zebras. They all looked perfect to me.

Paris has inspired photographers ever since Nicéphore Niépce and Louis Daguerre introduced the first camera in 1839. I was lucky enough to admire the works of Cartier-Bresson, Capa, Riboud, and many more extraordinary photographers when L'Hôtel de Ville de Paris showcased the Paris Magnum exhibit. The City Hall regularly hosts free art exhibits, an opportunity to visit some of the vast rooms and salons of the Neo-Renaissance building. On the Seine side, a small garden is open to the public and is home to a few chickens. The large square on the west side is converted into an outdoor skating rink during the winter months. A nice change from its historical purpose: the former Place de Grève was the favored site for public executions during the Old Régime. It's also the spot where the guillotine was first introduced in April 1792.

Hôtel de Ville de Paris
Place de l'Hôtel de Ville and rue de Lobau, 4th arr.

Roméo, Roméo wherefore art thou?

When I worked in Paris, the métro was a convenient way to get around but I did not exactly look forward to my long daily commute. If a seat was available, I quickly plunged into my book and tried to shut out the world around me. When I had to stand, I did my best to ignore the strangers who inevitably encroached upon my personal space. As an occasional user, I now approach public transportation like a social study. I spend time observing those strangers, eavesdropping on conversations, and trying to read their lives through the threads of their clothes. Once blind to my surroundings, I have become a spectator. Occasionally, I will even eschew proper French manners and engage verbally. As I exited the Bastille station on a lovely Sunday morning, I noticed a man sitting on the stairs. In front of him, a flattened cardboard box was covered with greens. In front of that, a well-behaved rabbit calmly stared at me while twitching his little nose. I was fresh out of carrots so I gave the man a few coins and inquired about the rabbit's name. "Roméo," he answered. We chatted for a couple of minutes. As I went on my way, I mused about the day when Roméo would meet his Juliet and overrun the métro with a growing herd of little Montagues and Capulets.

I can't promise you will meet Roméo and his friend around Bastille: some encounters happen by chance, never to be experienced again. Others are more permanent. The infamous Bastille prison was stormed and destroyed by the Parisians on July 14, 1789 but remnants of the fortress can still be found in a handful of locations, including the Bastille métro station. On the platform of Line 5, in direction of Bobigny, look for a piece of the wall that surrounded the moat.

Roméo and Friend
Bastille métro station, 4th arr.

The doctor will see you now

Gary's first trip to Paris had not started well. Within a couple of days, he was in the throes of a brutal asthma attack that kept him sleepless at night and miserable around the clock. He had not packed an inhaler, let alone a prescription. After an afternoon stroll in the Luxembourg gardens, the green cross of a pharmacy on rue Soufflot became our beacon: maybe we could get an OTC medication to provide him some relief. After hearing my plea, the helpful pharmacist wrote down an address on a piece of paper: "This doctor is only one block from here; he'll write you a prescription and I'll fill it," he said. "But it's almost 5 pm and we don't even have an appointment," I replied. "Just go to his office; he will take you in." A few minutes later, we stood across the Panthéon next to a massive wooden door. The gold plaque on the limestone wall read: *Psychanalyste, Psychiatre*. Mildly amusing, to say the least: the pharmacist had sent us to a shrink. But one cannot be a psychiatrist without a medical degree so I rang the bell and the door unlatched with a buzz. Although no one was there to greet us, we quickly found our way to an empty waiting room. After twenty minutes, a door opened and the doctor appeared. Gary was in need of an interpreter: we both stepped into the doctor's office while Rick and Raegan continued to peruse old issues of Elle and Paris Match. In case you are wondering, the patient did not lie down on the proverbial couch. The doctor fished out a stethoscope from his desk drawer and gave Gary a thorough check-up before writing up the *ordonnance*. A modest amount of money was exchanged. We shook hands. A prescription was filled. We all breathed better.

Sadly, "our" pharmacy closed its doors in 2014. Its original contents (wood paneling, glass jars, copper alembics, even the bronze cash register) have been transferred to the Musée Carnavalet. A smart clothing shop currently occupies the location on rue Soufflot; thankfully, it had to preserve the elegant 1857 exterior as the city distinguished Pharmacie Lhopitallier for its "most beautiful façade" forty years ago. Throughout Paris, you will undoubtedly notice many old shops that have been repurposed: just on the west side of the Luxembourg, look for Le Pont Traversé, a former butcher shop that is now home to a used bookstore.

Pharmacie Lhopitallier
3 rue Soufflot, 5th arr.

Look right, then left

Most commuters will agree that a single minute can make or break their day. In Paris, one develops an intimate relationship with a given métro line. You know exactly which car to board to be the closest to your exit or transfer point; you know when to hurry in the corridors and run on the escalators to catch your RER on time; you know when you missed your perfect connection and can spare five minutes to pick up Le Monde or listen to the lone cello player. And, in the rare instance when the métro becomes *aérien* and you briefly escape the bowels of the earth, you know when to look up from your book. Ligne 5 was my line. Between Gare de l'Est and Austerlitz, I would always sit –or stand– on the right side. Slowly leaving the sharply curved station of Quai de la Rapée on school mornings, the train would hug the brick walls of the morgue; ghastly neon lights shone behind frosted windows, only suggesting the mysterious or terrifying events of the night before. Just as suddenly, I would catch my first sight of the Viaduc d'Austerlitz over the Seine and the elevated entrance into the train station: within seconds, the dark cavern would swallow us whole, like the gaping mouth of a hungry giant.

Be aware that pedestrians are not allowed on the Viaduc d'Austerlitz. If you ride Ligne 5 toward Porte d'Italie, sit on the right to see the morgue, the curved tracks, the viaduct, the islands, Notre-Dame, and the dramatic entrance. On the left side, you can catch a glimpse of Les Docks-Cité de la Mode et du Design; it looks like a green caterpillar floating over the river. If on foot, take the steps down from Pont d'Austerlitz to Port Saint Bernard: you'll be rewarded with splendid views of the viaduct, a single steel arch spanning 460 feet. Plenty of colorful houseboats, too.

Viaduc d'Austerlitz from below pont d'Austerlitz
Place Valhubert, 5th arr.

Best laid plans

Location, location, location: I share the realtor's mantra when I book my accommodations. Imagine my dismay when Rick and I showed up at our hotel in the 11th arrondissement on a rainy February morning only to find out that *un bug informatique* had swallowed my prepaid reservation. Profuse apologies were offered and we were walked to another, nicer property in the 6th. Nothing against the Left Bank but I had already made plans on the other side of the river. Rick's usual cheerfulness did not alleviate my grumpiness, even after an excellent dinner: instead of an easy walk back to the hotel, we were now looking at an awkward métro itinerary with two changes. Tired but not sleepy yet, we decided to hoof it to Saint-Germain. My mood lifted almost immediately. The rain had stopped, the night was crisp, the crowds were sparse, and the city was putting out its best light show seemingly just for us. We let ourselves be guided by the illuminated monuments. As we got closer to the Seine, each landmark served as a beacon: Notre-Dame, la Conciergerie, l'Institut de France. We lingered on the *quais*, at the water's edge. Bright reflections danced on the rippled surface, creating a new tableau each time a boat cut through the river. Every bridge span framed dramatic scenes where shadow and light played hide-and-seek. Under the Pont Neuf, the varied expressions of the grotesque stone heads seemed to illustrate all the emotions of the day: it started as a bust and ended in a spectacular evening, courtesy of a computer bug.

Thirty-seven bridges cross the Seine in Paris. Pont Neuf, the oldest one, was built between 1578 and 1607 and it was indeed a novel bridge: the first one made of stone, the first one without houses along its sides, the first one with curbs to shield pedestrians from mud and horses. It crosses the whole river, at the western tip of the Ile de la Cité. The equestrian statue of Henri IV dominates the square du Vert-Galant, a green oasis in the middle of the city and the river.

Pont Neuf
Between quai de Conti and quai des Grands Augustins, 6th arr.

La conversation

– So, you wanted to tell me something?

– I'm thinking about publishing a book.

– What is it about?

– Well, it would be kind of a cross between a photography essay, a memoir, and a travel guide. Set in Paris. A bunch of little moments in Paris.

– Sounds very original.

– Maybe I'm just crazy. Do you think somebody would actually want to read a book like that?

– Look! Someone just did! They're holding it right now.

Do not expect to contemplate Etienne's sculpture next time you wander around place Saint-Sulpice: La Conversation was inaugurated in Havana, Cuba in 2012 and only made a brief appearance in Paris in 2014. It's the beauty of street art: always surprising, usually ephemeral. The church itself was started in the 17th century and construction continued for 200 years. After Notre-Dame, it is the largest church in Paris. Millions of Americans took note of it when Dan Brown published The Da Vinci Code: its gnomon, a marble obelisk used to determine the time of the equinoxes, drew crowds from all over the world. Also inside, a great organ and magnificent pulpit are worth a visit. With its mismatched towers and the sign above the main entrance still referencing it as a revolutionary place of worship for the "Supreme Being," Saint-Sulpice is indeed a very unusual church.

Eglise Saint-Sulpice
50 rue de Vaugirard, 6th arr.

ETIENNE
CONVERSATION

Death and life

We are the first visitors of the afternoon, contemplating aisles of glass curios, lined with glass shelves, covered with glass jars. Save for the occasional creaking of the wood floor, the room is eerily quiet. We speak in hushed tones while deciphering the yellowed handwritten labels on the jars detailing the condition of the patient whose specimen they contain. Musée d'Anatomie Pathologique Dupuytren is the "library" where aspiring doctors studied an incredibly vast compendium of diseases; samples have been gathered since the 17th century. We are literally surrounded by parts of dead people: deformed skeletons, globs of flesh soaking in formaldehyde, mummified heads. It is both unsettling and fascinating. On our way out, the curator explains that computers have replaced the physical handling of specimens, although a student will occasionally check out an item for personal study. He is a teaching medical professor as well. While appreciative of modern technology, he stresses the importance of not getting so caught up in the science of medicine that we forget the human experience: the smartest doctor is only as good as his ability to relate to the patient as a whole, not just to his pathology. I am filled with awe and respect: these human beings were often ridiculed as freaks while they were alive; they never knew how much they would ultimately contribute to the advancement of medicine. And I wonder how much of our humanity is lost when we watch a spine rotate on a computer screen instead of listening to a man in his wheelchair. Can virtual reality generate real empathy?

Viewing the Dupuytren museum was not for the faint of heart (it has closed its doors since my last visit and the entire collection was moved to the university campus at Jussieu.) It was located on the site where the Cordeliers Franciscan monks built a church, a convent, and a theology college in the 13th century. After chasing them away during the French revolution, Danton established his Club des Cordeliers in the chapel. Nowadays, art exhibits are shown in the 14th-century refectory. Strolling through the peaceful garden and the cloister, you will soon be confronted by Death, as sculpted by Allouard. Not to worry: a nearby bronze of Dr. Xavier Bichat is ready for a pitched battle for Life.

Faculté de médecine de Paris, campus des Cordeliers
15 rue de l'Ecole de Médecine, 6th arr.

Pretty dirty

The day had not started well. I had checked in at my two-star hotel near Montparnasse and the thoughtful receptionist had warned me that the elevator was *hors service*. *Temporairement. Je suis désolée.* I would need to haul my luggage to the *cinquième étage* which, you know, actually means the sixth floor here. I told myself I could use the exercise and started to climb the carpeted steps of a narrow staircase. When I reached my floor, I dropped the suitcase onto the landing and paused to catch my breath. Then, a magical sight: to my right, framed within the stairwell window, the Eiffel tower stretched above slate rooftops and brick chimneys. Wide bands of dirt on the glass looked like gauzy curtains that had been slightly pulled, just for me, to reveal an ethereal vision of the Iron Lady. I was in Paris. Everything was right again.

It just sneaks up on you. You're minding your own business around Montparnasse, checking out the bamboo grove in the parc de Belleville, or stepping out of the Air France bus at Les Invalides. You're not even close to the Trocadéro, nor in the vicinity of the Champ de Mars and it suddenly appears in all its graceful might: there's no escaping the Eiffel Tower when you are in Paris. I always enjoy those surprise sightings but if you're looking for some picture-perfect locations, try the views from place de Breteuil, square Rapp, or on rue de l'Alboni near the Passy métro station.

Eiffel Tower
Quai Branly, 7th arr.

Golden dome

Mom and I were strolling along the East side of Les Invalides when the sun unexpectedly pierced through a canopy of gray clouds and illuminated the gilded cupola adjacent to the Saint-Louis cathedral. Like a precious ring set in a satin jewelry box, the gleaming dome of the royal chapel emerged from the bronze foliage of regimented trees lining the boulevard. We both looked up, slightly stunned by the sudden show that seemed to be perfectly timed for our arrival. "Your grandfather loved Napoléon," Mom said with a slight break in her voice. The dome marks the final resting place of *L'Empereur* and the proximity of Napoléon's grave had reopened the old wound that would never heal: she lost her beloved father when she was merely thirty-four years old. Grandpa was a WWI veteran and a huge admirer of Napoléon I: had René been born a hundred years earlier, I imagine he would have joined the ranks of faithful *grognards* who followed their general from Egypt to Russia. I glanced at my mother but said nothing. I took her hand, gave it a gentle squeeze. We pressed on to the Rodin Museum in silence.

Don't get intimidated by the dozens of antique canons lined up along the moat or by the expansiveness of Les Invalides. Louis XIV ordered the construction of this hospice for war veterans in 1670. Although it was completed in eight short years, it's almost a city in itself: the building complex includes a hospital and a retirement home for veterans, two churches, gardens, the residence and offices of the Military Governor of Paris, monuments, tombs, several museums covering centuries of military art from medieval armors to WWII tanks, and Napoléon's stuffed horse. The Emperor's crypt below the golden dome draws large crowds. Sometimes, the best show takes place in the Cour d'Honneur that Chateaubriand described as a "military cloister:" it is often used as rehearsal grounds for military exercises.

Hôtel National des Invalides
129 rue de Grenelle, 7th arr.

Carless

I just had to be there. Summertime is not my favorite season in Paris but this would be a once-in-a-lifetime experience. On July 14, 1989 Rick and I lined up behind steel barricades near rue de Berri to watch an extravaganza of a parade. The avenue des Champs-Elysées was closed to traffic for the whole day and one million people had gathered along one mile of pavement to celebrate the Bicentennial of the French Revolution. The evening parade opened with a huge steam locomotive, followed by French floats brimming with regional musicians, Africans beating on steel drums, British marching under artificial rain, a Russian ballerina skating on real ice, Chinese students pushing their bicycles, and the Florida A&M band moon-walking to the sound of James Brown's greatest hits. For sheer visual pleasure, nothing could beat the towering *valseuses*: with electric cars hidden under their immense black dresses, they gracefully glided and waltzed while holding children in their arms. Suddenly, the drumming stopped and the marchers stood still. A powerful female voice cut through the night and silenced the reveling crowd. Soaring a cappella notes enveloped us like a soft blanket of fog: Jessye Norman was singing La Marseillaise. For several minutes it felt like we all shared one collective heartbeat, one same emotion. Cheeks glistened from tears. Heads of States watched the soprano's performance from the gilded salons of the Hôtel de la Marine at la Concorde but we, the people, flooded the Champs-Elysées just like our ancestors who took to the streets two hundred years before. This time, it was not a revolution: *juste une grande fête.*

On September 27th, 2015 I went back to Les Champs for another parade of sorts. Once again, the avenue was closed to traffic and filled with a sea of exuberant humans. The Paris Mayor had decreed that day to be the first time for "Paris sans Voiture," an event that is now repeated every first Sunday of the month: pedestrians own ten lanes of cobblestones, along with cyclists, roller skaters, and the occasional hoverboard. The upper part of the avenue channels the crowd between two rows of buildings, fancy shops, and restaurants. Without cars, the lower part (between the Rond-Point and Concorde) looks like a giant park with people spilling into the gardens on both sides.

Avenue des Champs-Elysées
Between place de la Concorde and place Charles de Gaulle, 8th arr.

Lèche-vitrine

My first serious attempt at baking proved to be a minor *désastre*. With extended family coming over for a Saturday night dinner, I confidently informed my mother that I would take charge of dessert. Forty-five years later, the mere mention of my *tarte basque* still elicits eye rolls and hilarity: it sure looked good but, in general, one does not wish to have a chainsaw at hand to slice a pie. I eventually gained experience in the kitchen and can handle savory dishes with gusto but, to this day, baking remains my Achilles heel. That may explain my inordinate fascination with French pastry shops: I feast my eyes on intricate chocolate sculptures, elaborate cakes worthy of an art museum, rows next to rows of perfect eclairs, tartlets, and meringues… *Lèche-vitrine* often ranks as a national sport in France but I'll take a window display at Ladurée over the designer shops on avenue Montaigne any day of the week. Besides, the instant gratification of a licorice macaron only sets me back a couple of euros!

Ladurée is generally credited with inventing the double-decker macaron where ganache, buttercream, or jam is sandwiched between two small almond meringues. They are properly referred to as "macarons parisiens" since the word also designates other types of cookies that often include coconut. Ladurée always assigns at least one window to macaron art, varying the displays and the colors with the seasons. You will find the flagship store in the 8th arrondissement but the shop on rue Bonaparte in the 6th is conveniently located on the same street as Pierre Hermé and five minutes away from Gérard Mulot. All three houses contend for the title of best macaron baker: I suggest you pick up samples at each shop, find a bench in square Laurent Prache next to the St-Germain-des-Prés church, and conduct your very own blind tasting.

Ladurée
18 rue Royale, 8th arr.

Le Nozze di Figaro

There was the magician who lit a fire into his top hat and extinguished it with a clap. There was the zoologist who brought a huge shiny python and allowed us to pet it. And there was the fairy-like harpist, dressed in an ethereal white gown, who released dreamy music out of the largest instrument I had ever seen. When I was at the *école maternelle*, entertainment and culture came to us. Once I "graduated" to the *école primaire*, a field trip bus took me and my school friends to the Opéra: two dozen kids, Madame Collin, and a few chaperones to attend a performance of The Marriage of Figaro. Of course, we got the cheap seats at the *poulailler*; the seats that are so far from the stage and so high up in the theater that you feel you can almost touch the ceiling. Oh, that wondrous ceiling! The Italian libretto went right over my head and the beautiful costumes could not sustain my interest for three hours but Chagall's ceiling mesmerized me, drew me in and made me want to take flight. To have wings and touch the sky…

To describe the Opéra Garnier as opulent is a mild understatement. The marble double staircase sets the tone and leads to rotundas, salons, and a foyer showcasing mosaics, tapestries, chandeliers, windows, and mirrors worthy of Versailles. And a lot of gold! Get yourself a ticket to a performance, settle into your red velvet seat, admire Chagall's ceiling, and take advantage of the intermission to sip a flute of Champagne by the stone balustrade at night, watching the rooftops of the Avenue de l'Opéra toward the Louvre. You are unlikely to meet the famous Phantom and, short of training with Paris firemen, you will not get access to the underground lake, a vaulted water tank located 33 feet below the stage and matching its dimensions. Its purpose? When architect Charles Garnier realized that the site was swampy, he decided to fight water with water: a huge filled tank would neutralize the pressure from the waterlogged soil.

Opéra Garnier, from the terrace of Le Printemps department store
Place de l'Opéra, 9th arr.

The choir

Faced with the unenviable challenge of teaching music to twenty-five children, Mademoiselle Fangouse quickly realized the limits of what she could accomplish with her allotted weekly hour. Letting us take turns on the lonely straight piano in the music room would surely plunge the whole class into chaos. The only realistic path to sanity was to involve us in one collective activity, using the sole instruments that did not require funding by the *Education Nationale*: our voices. She rearranged the class in two vocal groups, expertly commandeered the piano, and conducted us with the unashamed animation of a real maestro. Shubert's The Trout was on the menu, along with a few other classics. She did not reveal her master plan until January. The year would conclude with a field trip: a meeting with dozens of other classes to join them in a gigantic choir. In Paris!

From boulevard des Capucines, the bus slowly turned right into a cobblestone courtyard: we had finally arrived. Under the watchful eyes of our chaperones, we eagerly left our seats and lined up in front of Théâtre Edouard VII. Trepidation was brewing in my heart: I had been to the theater before but this time would be different. This time I would be performing. Along with another six hundred middle schoolers. As we entered the theater, we were directed to our respective sections: high voices stage left, low voices stage right. A few musicians already occupied the stage. We stood in front of our luxurious velour seats. The master conductor brought the choir to order. Silence first, voices next. That day, we all made beautiful music and Mademoiselle Fangouse beamed with pride.

Built in 1913, the Edouard VII theater stands apart because of its stately location. Tucked into a quiet street off the grands boulevards, between the Opéra Garnier and the Madeleine, the somewhat intimate venue (720 seats) also boasts a plush restaurant and bar accessible to all. Facing the English king's equestrian statue, the terrace offers a quiet break from the bustle of shopping at les grands magasins nearby.

Théâtre Edouard VII
10 place Edouard VII, 9th arr.

It's the journey

Oh, how I love train travel! Surely genetics factor in: both my grandfathers were *cheminots* —they worked for the railroads— and neither of them ever owned a car. What a treat when Grandma Régine came to Paris before a school holiday to take me to Royan by train! After climbing into our 2nd Class steel rail car, she and I would settle in the compartment we would occupy for the next six hours: twin dark green vinyl bench seats shared by eight people, framed black and white SNCF photographs above each numbered *place*, steel luggage racks at the top. I always claimed the spot by the window not just to watch the scenery but because of the fold-down tray on the side where I could park my coloring book, my pencils, a deck of cards. At some point, the "table" had to be cleared for lunch. Régine would extract a couple of *sandwichs jambon-beurre* from her bag, along with fruit, water, and a package of cookies. Good manners required that cookies be offered to other passengers as well. Conversations were started. Newspapers and magazines were swapped. Knitting needles and balls of yarn appeared. Windows could be rolled down and, sometimes, the multilingual posted sign "It is dangerous to lean out" was ignored. Bliss.

If your idea of train travel encompasses more than a tray table and a ham sandwich, the Orient-Express may strike a chord. Yes, the legendary train rides again, complete with vintage —but luxurious— cabins, gastronomic cuisine, sublime scenery, alluring destinations, and windows that still roll down. London, Berlin, Istanbul, Venice: what a civilized way to reach the great cities of Europe! If a journey on the famous Art Deco train is not in the cards, pop into Gare de l'Est between March and November: perhaps you'll want to gawk at the gleaming blue and gold coaches of the Venice Simplon Orient-Express parked at the platform. And dream.

Gare de l'Est
Place du 11 novembre 1918, 10th arr.

Art in a cup of tea

Julien had become my restaurant of choice. A classic brasserie in a rapidly gentrifying neighborhood, it was the perfect place to meet up with my Parisian cousins or to introduce American friends to classic French cuisine in stunning Art Nouveau surroundings. On a previous visit with Mom, our dinner there proved even more memorable when, halfway through the meal, we discovered that the snail-loving gentleman sitting next to her on the banquette was, in fact, one of my customers in the US. What were the odds?

I was alone this time. After a dessert of profiteroles, I ordered my usual *verveine-menthe*: I wanted to linger for a while and observe the mesmerizing ballet of precise waiters and *chefs de rang*, a flurry of black slacks and white shirts waltzing from table to table. I poured my tea into the dainty porcelain cup and let it cool. Then, an extraordinary sight: the reflection of the intricate glass ceiling appeared, a blue and green flower perfectly centered on the surface of the tranquil brew. I smiled and stared at my cup, marveling at the serendipity, wanting to etch this vision in my mind forever. It felt like a Proustian moment in the making.

Brasserie Julien is classified as a historical monument: the building dates from 1903 and its remarkable decor showcases the creativity and skills of Parisian artists at the turn of the century. Charles Buffet's glass ceiling panels are framed by ornate crown molding and filter natural light in the dining room. Glass flowers, peacocks, and nymphs designed by masters Armand Ségaud and Louis Trézel play hide-and-seek on monumental mirrors; the deep, curvy mahogany bar is topped with traditional zinc; the ceramic patterns on the tile floor echo the floral motif of the glass canopies. A jewel. Sit at table #24, Edith Piaf's favorite, and hum La Vie en Rose.

Brasserie Julien
16 rue du Faubourg-Saint-Denis, 10th arr.

Christmas circus

A dozen burly men were huddled at the curb, spilling on both sides of the massive burgundy doorway. Dressed in overalls, t-shirts, and heavy boots they were dragging on their cigarettes and chatting between puffs. The sign above the door read *Entrée du Personnel*. Clearly, they were on break from work. They looked out of place in Paris, especially at the edge of the posh Marais neighborhood. Suddenly, I caught a distinctive whiff: the circus smell, that funky mix of sweat, urine, and sawdust. I walked around the corner, past a string of narrow bars and cafés, and there it stood: the majestic Cirque d'Hiver, a yellow rotunda festooned like a tiered birthday cake. The building itself had not made an impression on me in my youth. Dad's company offered complimentary tickets to a performance every December: we had attended many times but I guess I was more enthralled by the circus acts than its architecture. I sat on a bench on tiny place Pasdeloup and an old film started to play in my brain: Achille Zavatta with his red nose and clown horn; the rider in a gold tutu standing on a galloping horse; the leotard-clad gymnast with chalky hands flying from one trapeze to the other; and the highlight of the show, at least for me: the plate spinners! For a brief moment, I felt eight years old again.

Paris already had a "summer" circus in the gardens of the Champs-Elysées but its manager convinced Jacques-Ignace Hittorff, the city Chief Architect, to build a new circus so his troupe would have a permanent home during the winter months. Cirque Napoléon officially opened in 1852 and was named after Napoléon III. It was permanently renamed Cirque d'Hiver in 1872. The Bouglione family produces a new show every year with performances from mid-October to mid-March. The circus is also used for other events: theater, concerts, and the occasional fashion show or political meeting. A couple of doors down, take a peek at Le Clown Bar, an idiosyncratic restaurant decorated with Belle Epoque ceramic tiles depicting classic clowns.

Cirque d'Hiver
110 Rue Amelot, 11th Arr.

Fromage et dessert

During the mid-Sixties, my father sometimes traveled internationally for work: England, Sweden, the USA… He spent four months in Arizona in 1964 and nourished my own dream of visiting America some day. When the company sent him to Phoenix again three years later, my mother joined him for a month while my grandparents took care of my sister and me. Although she did not speak any English, Mom was excited to discover a new country and her letters to us were generally enthusiastic. However, she was stymied by a couple of unfortunate realities: the desert heat in August and the absence of real cheese. Like many French people, she is of the creed that "a meal without cheese is not a meal;" white and yellow bricks of dairy products just could not rival the extensive and flavorful selection we had at home. Her distress was so palpable that we wanted to appease her longing. Françoise and I knew we could not send her the French cheeses she craved so much but we did the next best thing: we mailed her the labels from a few Camembert boxes. I know our hearts were in the right place but I am not sure we were completely helpful.

Cheese is an integral part of our French dining experience and often showcased as a separate course on restaurant menus: a typical 4-course dinner will include cheese and dessert. Depending on the establishment, the cheese course is already plated or may be presented as a plateau de fromages. In that case, the server will cut pieces from two or three cheeses of your choice. It's generally considered a bit "gauche" to request more than three. And then, there is Astier in the 11th arrondissement where a Gargantua-worthy cheese platter is brought to your table and actually stays on your table. For a while. Without a waiter standing nearby. So you can sample many varieties. And have second helpings of your favorites. It's my mother's idea of heaven.

Cheese platter, Restaurant Astier
44 rue Jean-Pierre Timbaud, 11th arr.

Painted Ladies

My first trip to San Francisco was glorious. Like any wide-eyed French girl who grew up watching Hollywood films and American series on TV, I just couldn't get enough of the amazing sights that already felt so familiar: the majestic Golden Gate bridge, the white walls of Alcatraz surrounded by the scintillating bay waters, those hills that Steve McQueen had made so famous in Bullitt... We took the ferry to Sausalito, we rode the cable cars, we drove down the sharp turns of the "crookedest street." But we also discovered several areas that had not registered in our mental check list. One such surprise was the Painted Ladies of San Francisco, a group of pastel colored Victorian houses facing Alamo Square. The nearly identical facades in pale pink, blue, and yellow seemed to reflect the essence of California: sunny, colorful, whimsical. Many years later, as I was wandering around Gare de Lyon, I had to do a double take. Stumbling upon rue Crémieux, I found myself staring at two rows of stunning houses: the gray cobbled street was lined with pastel-colored homes, all of a similar architectural style. Flower boxes were tastefully set on the curb; painted birds, cats, and trompe-l'oeil foliage decorated the walls; bikes leaned below the windows and indifferent cats minded their own business. Surrounded by Haussmannian buildings, I had found a piece of California: another row of Painted Ladies right in the middle of Paris.

Rue Crémieux is arguably the most colorful street in Paris. Opened in 1865, it is composed of 35 homes modeled after the blue-collar housing of that era, where all homes shared a similar exterior appearance and floor plan: a kitchen in the basement and six rooms on two stories. Although the pedestrian street covers less than 450 feet in length, it is so distinctive and bucolic that you feel transported to a Mediterranean village. Don't miss the murals on the corner of rue de Bercy.

Rue Crémieux
Between rue de Bercy and rue de Lyon, 12th arr.

Baba

There was a ritual: the trip to the *pâtisserie* with my mother and my sister on Sunday morning. We would choose four *petits gâteaux*: Mom usually picked a *millefeuilles* for herself while Françoise and I would flip flop between the *éclair au chocolat* and the *tartelette aux cerises*. A *baba au rhum* was always selected for Dad. The lady behind the counter would delicately grab the pastries with her wide metal tongs and gently position them on a white cardboard square. She would fold the scored edges so that the pastries could not slide off; get a wide sheet of fancy paper and wrap the whole thing in such a way that the package looked like a pyramid, secured on all four sides with a thin, colorful ribbon; then pinch the top and tie the ribbon to make a small loop that doubled as a carrying handle. Every shop wrapped their pastries with the same care, the same style, the same elegance, and everybody went home carrying paper pyramids hiding delicious pastries. I must have been about twenty years old when, after Sunday lunch, Dad declared that he didn't care for *babas au rhum*. We were stupefied or, as the French aptly say, *nous sommes restés baba*. "But you've eaten them every Sunday for 25 years," said Mom! "Because you've bought them every Sunday for 25 years", Dad replied! "I'd much rather have a *chou à la crème*." I have not seen a *baba au rhum* in the house since then.

I can't recall when I last saw one of those pyramidal packages. They seem to have been replaced with generic (or fancy) lidded cardboard boxes. But the pastries are still there which, of course, is the most important! Paris certainly does not suffer from a lack of sumptuous pastry shops; some of them have crafted pastries for centuries. But eating habits have changed and les petits gâteaux are not just a Sunday treat anymore. Beyond the fancy salons de thé, many pâtisseries set up a few tables and chairs to encourage on-site sampling, a lovely way to take a break from shopping and sightseeing. In addition to true artisan bread and delicious pastries (try the Paris-Brest), Boulangerie BO offers the pleasure of sitting next to a magnificent façade.

Boulangerie BO
85 bis rue de Charenton, 12th arr.

I'll never get lost

Shortly after they were married in 1922, Marie-Louise and Albert left the small family farm in southern France and took the train to Paris. They both were the first (and only) members of their respective families to leave the countryside and "choose" the city life: necessity motivated their decision. Arriving at the Austerlitz station, they rented a small hotel room on rue du Chevaleret and lived there for several years. He worked for the *Compagnie du chemin de fer de Paris à Orléans*, she was a housekeeper. When my father was born, they moved into a small apartment in Ivry-sur-Seine, a city bordering Paris to the South. Eventually, they retired and took the train back to the farm. Grandma cherished her memories of their years in Paris: she loved the sophistication, the clothes, the pace. She often told me: "I was never afraid of getting lost in Paris. All I had to do was follow the Seine upstream until I could see the Ivry fort. From there, I always knew my way home." I'll never get lost either.

My grandmother wouldn't recognize her neighborhood these days. Over the past twenty years, this whole area of the 13th arrondissement has been utterly transformed while making space for the construction of the Bibliothèque Nationale de France; it was inaugurated in 1996. Situated one block from the Library, rue du Chevaleret is now lined with very modern apartments, offices, and shopping centers. But the Library still offers beautiful views of her beloved Seine.

Passerelle Simone de Beauvoir and BNF François Mitterand
Quai François Mauriac, 13th arr.

Murphy

Summer 1993. Rick and I were standing below the mechanical schedule board at the Austerlitz station, waiting for a new clickety-clack to find out the platform number for our train to Gourdon. Suddenly, Rick exclaimed: "Look! It's Murphy! Murphy Brown. From TV! She's at the newsstand." There was no mistake. The hair, the height, the posture: Candice Bergen was indeed standing at Relais H, twenty feet from us. I noticed the little girl next to her. She appeared to be six or seven years old; she was wearing a white summer dress and a brimmed straw hat. It had to be her daughter Chloe. I had read Vanity Fair's recent piece on Bergen; the article covered her hit show and VP Dan Quayle's comments on family values, the childhood she shared with her ventriloquist dad's wooden dummy, and her current family life. A picture of Chloe was included. I looked around hoping to spot her husband Louis Malle. He was an iconic French director and one of my favorites since the release of Lacombe Lucien, a haunting film taking place in southwestern France during the German Occupation. I knew he owned a country house near Cahors; it made perfect sense that the family would be catching a train at Austerlitz. On our way to the platform, I made eye contact with "Murphy" and quietly told her I loved her show. She had no entourage; she seemed a bit surprised to be sighted in a French train station. She nodded a thank you. Shortly after, she and Chloe boarded the last car of our train. For a few hours, I traveled with a movie star.

Austerlitz is one of the six major train stations in Paris but it doesn't currently host any TGV (high speed) service, which has led to declining traffic. It is also the last one to undergo extensive renovation. Particularly noteworthy is the steel and glass hall: built in 1867, it is the second largest in France (925 feet in length). The current renovation project will restore this impressive verrière but it will no longer cover railroad tracks: instead, it will be converted into a shopping galleria.

Gare d'Austerlitz
85 quai d'Austerlitz, 13th Arr.

Café culture

My café was not listed in any guidebook. There was not even a terrace to watch people —and the world— go by. A little hole in the wall, Le Village on rue de la Montagne Sainte-Geneviève was your typical *Bar-Tabac* where one bought cigarettes, gum, and lotto tickets while nursing a glass of cheap red wine or a cup of strong coffee. It could barely accommodate twenty bodies but had the distinct advantage of sitting a couple of minutes away from Lycée Henri IV: within a couple of weeks, it had become my inevitable morning stop before class. Marie-Aude was always the first one to arrive: she caught an early train from Melun. I would find her at her usual spot, sitting on the vinyl *banquette* and sipping her *grand crème*. Thierry and Olivier would arrive a bit later and drop a few francs in the pinball machine before joining us around the square Formica table. Guys smoked French Gauloises, girls smoked American *blondes*. I smoked nothing but carried a Bic lighter in my purse anyway because someone always asked for a match: just like cavemen in prehistoric times, sharing fire was a convivial gesture and I did not want to be left out. Conversations quickly jumped from math to music, politics to film, philosophy to philosophy. We were young and full of self-importance. At five minutes before eight, after the last sip and the last drag, we would climb the last fifty yards to the school courtyard. The ritual repeated itself after lunch and we reinvented the world yet again.

What makes the café experience so special in Paris is the feeling that time is suspended: how often do you give yourself one hour to watch complete strangers, eavesdrop on their conversations, linger with an espresso, a book, or a friend? Like most neighborhood cafés, Le Village never reached mythical status (I checked it out recently: it now serves a nice selection of cocktails; no pinball, though.) But the Left Bank is home to several iconic cafés and brasseries where artists and intellectuals hung out between 1910 and 1940. In the Montparnasse area, Picasso, Modigliani, Man Ray, Hemingway, Henri Miller, Oscar Wilde, Verlaine, Apollinaire, Sartre, and countless others ate, drank and talked at La Rotonde, La Coupole, Le Dôme, and Le Select. They happen to be within minutes of each other, making for an easy pilgrimage. Their illustrious patrons enlightened the world; their retro neon signs now illuminate the night.

Brasseries in Montparnasse
99, 102, 105, 108 boulevard du Montparnasse, 14th arr.

The sensible thing

Paris became my world after my high school graduation: for the first time, I was actually studying in Paris intra muros. My introduction to college life started with the inevitable *bizutage*, the long-held tradition of hazing newbies. Business school students were not particularly imaginative in that department: our public humiliation was confined to performing a series of pushups in front of the funeral parlor on the south side of the Panthéon (*faites des pompes devant les pompes funèbres*: French speakers will appreciate our lame attempt at humor.) Meanwhile, our friends in Pharmacy school would regale us with scary tales of their spending dark hours in the Catacombs after being dropped in through a secret passage under their campus. In all cases, the sensible thing to do was to lay low and avoid becoming a target for the tormentors. Since Pharmacy was not my calling, I discovered the Catacombs on my own, long before they emerged as a popular attraction. Nowadays, a constant line of visitors snakes around place Denfert-Rochereau, all the way to the official entrance. In spite of stern warnings that *les personnes sensibles* (sensitive individuals) should reconsider entering the Empire of Death, nobody seems to turn back. There is a defibrillator unit by the cashier's booth but the sensible thing would be to set it up at the end of the long and dark underground tunnel: entering the ossuary where the bones of six million Parisians are neatly stacked against the walls is not for the faint of heart.

The Paris catacombs started out as quarries in Gallo-Roman times. It is estimated their overall area represents close to 40% of the surface of the city, although just a tiny portion is open to the public. In the 18th century, some Parisians cemeteries were dangerously overflowing: a decision was made to close them and transfer all remains to the underground galleries below the 14th arrondissement, starting with nightly convoys between cimetière des Innocents and avenue René Coty. Over the course of several decades, seventeen cemeteries were emptied out. Among the famous "residents:" literary giants Rabelais, Pascal, and Montesquieu. Many revolutionary figures who lost their heads at the guillotine are also spending eternity together in the Catacombs, including Marat and his assassin Charlotte Corday. What a strange twist of fate.

Catacombs
Place Denfert-Rochereau, 14th arr.

Out of mind, out of sight

For all the beauty in Paris, there is one universally loathed landmark: la Tour Montparnasse. It was not meant to be a monument but it seems impossible to ignore: the monstrous disruptor spoils the classic elegance of Parisian architecture. When I took classes on rue de Rennes, I caught a glimpse of the tower every morning as I exited the métro at St. Placide. My friends and I regularly walked up the street to buy books at the FNAC or have lunch at our favorite *crêperie*. Although the dark, massive skyscraper loomed tall over the train station and dwarfed the shopping mall below, we never paid attention to it. After a couple of weeks, it had simply become invisible to us. Isn't it funny how your mind so readily tunes out the familiar?

A few years ago, I booked a hotel room on rue de l'Arrivée. It did not even occur to me it would be situated right across the tower. After settling in on the 5th floor, I looked through the window: the imposing glass monolith occupied my whole field of vision. No lovely view of the Paris rooftops inviting me to pull out the drapes and gaze outside: I was facing a continuous wall of black rectangles divided by narrow strips of metal. I sighed. I opened the window for fresh air. It was early in the day and the sun was not at full zenith. I looked out and was treated to a surprising sight. The unseemly tower had morphed into a perfectly reflective surface: bathed in golden hues, a whole street of stone walls, slate roofs, zinc gutters, and vintage lamp posts suddenly was on full display. Paris was as beautiful as ever.

After the Eiffel Tower, Tour Montparnasse is the second tallest building within the city limits. Mostly occupied by offices, the skyscraper was widely considered an urban mistake and, two years after its completion in 1973, Paris passed a law to ban any construction taller than seven stories. In the eyes of many visitors, the tower only has two redeeming qualities: a restaurant on the 56th floor and an observation terrace on the top floor. They both deliver fantastic panoramas of Paris and beyond. Without the tower marring the view.

Tour Montparnasse
33 avenue du Maine, 15th arr.

It was a dark and stormy night

My sister made her grand –and loud– entrance into this world on a March afternoon. When Dad and I left the clinic, we headed out to have dinner at his sister's house. He was driving our beloved 2 CV Citroën, his very first car. I was riding in the front seat next to him and, being a few months shy of my third birthday, I was not even tall enough to see the road. The sun had set early and it was already pitch dark. Looking up through the side window, I could only make out the tops of a long line of sycamore trees. As we drove down the avenue, bright street lamps would briefly shine a light on them and the trees seemed to flicker at regular intervals just like hypnotic black and white images projected by a magic lantern. I started to doze off. Suddenly, a thunderous noise startled me and a hailstorm of tiny glass pieces rained on us: the windshield had exploded. I quickly ducked and curled into a ball under the dashboard. I stayed there until we pulled in front of Maguy's house a couple of minutes later. I emerged in tears, not out of fear but because I was upset: "They broke Daddy's car," I cried! I had no idea who "they" were. Maguy took me in her arms and comforted me. I spent the night at her house. That night, my aunt was my mother.

It's hard to believe that all Citroën cars were manufactured in Paris proper as late as 1970! Dad's 2 CV was born on the assembly line of the Citroën plan on quai de Javel, now quai André Citroën. That facility on the Left Bank closed in 1975. Its former site is now occupied by modern office buildings and a gorgeous 35-acre park that includes greenhouses, fountains, themed gardens, a reflecting pool, and even a tethered helium balloon that 30 passengers can ride to enjoy jaw-dropping views of the river, the Eiffel Tower, Notre-Dame, and the Sacré-Coeur.

Parc André Citroën
2 rue Cauchy, 15th arr.

The great escape

During the early Eighties, I spent nine months in the 16th arrondissement without venturing away from my workplace. Squandering two and a half hours in public transportation every day, I quickly settled into the much-lamented routine of *métro-boulot-dodo*. To think that my office was only minutes away from Le Corbusier's workshop on rue Nungesser or from the architectural treasures that Hector Guimard dreamed up on rue de La Fontaine! It did not even occur to me to get off the métro at Trocadéro, just once, and take in the spectacular view of the Iron Lady on a crisp winter morning when the plaza is deserted. I suppose that, unconsciously, I was already breaking away from my childhood and my native country. The California siren song was too loud to tune out: I would soon get married and start a new chapter in my life. Granted, the haughty *Seizième* was a far cry from the exuberant Latin Quarter I loved so much but I am a little bit sorry that I so easily surrendered to escapism. If life reveals itself like a mosaic of fleeting moments, I probably overlooked a few tiles, and a few gems, along the wide boulevards of the 16th.

Honoré de Balzac also had an escape plan from his home in Passy, a village that was absorbed into the 16th arrondissement in 1860. He wrote several novels and edited La Comédie Humaine during his seven years on rue Raynouard while trying to avoid his creditors: a hidden passage could lead him two floors down to tiny rue Berton for a quick disappearing act. His quaint house —now a museum— is not representative of the prevalent architecture in the district but serves as a reminder that the outer arrondissements of Paris once were a collection of villages. Signs of their original character is always a pleasant surprise.

Maison de Balzac
47 rue Raynouart, 16th arr.

Roundabout

I still prefer to call it *la place de l'Étoile*. I mean no disrespect to general de Gaulle but, really, could there have been a better name for the most famous roundabout in the world? With twelve large avenues converging toward its center like spokes on a giant wheel and hundreds of cars zipping around the imposing *Arc de Triomphe*, the square truly deserves Star status. My first spin around *l'Étoile* as a novice driver was exhilarating. I reasoned it would be my ultimate test: neither failure nor fender-bender was an option. Approaching from *porte Maillot*, I stared at my foe looming at the top of *avenue de la Grande-Armée*. I gripped the wheel of Mom's green Citroën Ami 6 and resolutely matched my speed to the other vehicles. Reaching the entrance of the roundabout, I negotiated my merge with aplomb but gingerly stayed on the outside perimeter for a 270° counterclockwise lap around the monument. When I slowly turned onto *avenue de Wagram* several minutes later, I was filled with relief and pride: I had conquered the Arc, unbeknown to my American passengers who never considered I might be just as apprehensive as they were.

If you ever desire to go on a thrill ride and circle l'Arc de Triomphe by car, be aware that drivers entering the roundabout have the right of way! Reaching the center of the square by foot is another conquest of a sort: you must walk through the passage du Souvenir, a fairly dark pedestrian tunnel that links avenue des Champs-Elysées and avenue de la Grande-Armée while providing access to the Tomb of the Unknown Soldier. Prepare to brave a tsunami of people who use the tunnel as a shortcut to cross the monumental square: its perimeter measures close to half a mile. Once at the base of the Arc, visitors can climb a narrow spiral staircase of 284 steps to reach the terrace and enjoy a spectacular view that encompasses all of Paris.

Arc de Triomphe
Place Charles de Gaulle, 17th arr.

Le chabrot

I must have been six years old when my lips touched wine for the first time. Dinner at my grandparents' farm always started with a country-style soup. Marie-Louise made a flavorful broth from a chicken carcass or a ham bone, added vegetables from the garden and a thick slice of bread: it was *la soupe au pain*. My cousin and I set the table at 6:45 pm sharp; fifteen minutes later, everybody was seated at the round kitchen table and hot soup was ladled into deep plates. For a while, the only sounds heard were those of metal spoons clanging against earthenware and some occasional slurping by little girls who were still learning their manners. We kept our eyes on grandpa Albert, synchronizing our eating speed with his, making sure we did not finish before him. When there was only half a cup of broth left in his plate, he would reach for the bottle of *vin rouge* from his own vineyard, stir half a cup of wine into his soup, and drink the mixture straight from the plate. *"On veut faire chabrot comme pépé!"* Christine and I would exclaim, begging grandma to pour a drop of wine into our plates as well. The broth turned a delicate pale pink, the indisputable proof that we were on our way to adulthood. Grabbing the flat rim of our plates with our small hands, we drank our chabrot. Just like Grandpa.

It's very unlikely that you will enjoy a chabrot in Paris: this practice is only observed in a few rural areas of France. There are still four main vineyards within the city limits: the oldest and largest one is in Montmartre (18th), the others are located in Parc de Belleville (20th), Parc de Bercy (12th), and Parc Georges-Brassens (15th.) Production is too small for Parisian wine to be served anywhere but oenophiles will not feel deprived: hipster wine bars have opened all over the city and neighborhood bistros continue to offer inexpensive, underrated glasses of red, white, and rosé. It's part of the culture, the soul, and even the art of Paris.

Caves du Chalet
22 rue des Dames, 17th arr.

Agility

Rick and I needed a finishing touch for the dining room. Some artwork that would fit in the niche above the fireplace mantle. Something that would be appropriate, and possibly inspiring, since it would face our guests at the dinner table. After unsuccessful ventures into art shows and poster shops, it suddenly dawned on me: how about a print of le Lapin Agile, the famous painting that adorns a wood panel on the façade of the namesake cabaret? A stylish rabbit sporting a tall blue cap and a frilly red sash, jumping out of a shiny copper kettle, balancing a bottle of wine on the back of his front paw: it would be perfect. A couple of months later, I was heading to the Montmartre museum, fully expecting to purchase my lithograph. *"Ah non, madame, nous n'en avons pas."* I was crushed with disappointment and could not fathom being satisfied with anything else. Back in the US, I pondered our next move: perhaps we could commission our artist friend Waveney to paint a full-size oil from a small photograph of the nimble rabbit? She was easily persuaded and, now, my daily breakfast includes a cup of tea and a little piece of Montmartre.

Founded in 1860, the Montmartre establishment did not acquire its famous name until 1875 when artist André Gill painted the rabbit sign. It was quickly referred to as Le Lapin à Gill and evolved to Au Lapin Agile, a clever and fitting pun. Along with Le Moulin-Rouge and Le Chat Noir, the cabaret became a favorite meeting place for artists and bohemians: Picasso, Renoir, Utrillo, and Van Gogh were regulars. To this day, it continues the tradition of presenting a show of French songs (and drinks) six nights a week. It is located right across from the vineyard of Montmartre.

Au Lapin Agile
22 rue des Saules, 18th arr.

Rags

My grandmother was a formidable seamstress who could take apart an old coat, flip the components, and sew it back to construct a new garment that mirrored the original. Her *talents de couturière* served her well during WWII. Sadly, my first foray into the world of fashion design quickly confirmed the genetics fairy did not bestow any aptitude for sewing when I was conceived. Tasked by my middle school teacher to cut and assemble a baby anorak, I reluctantly accompanied my mother to Marché Saint-Pierre to gather our supplies. Contemplating long rows of fabric bolts neatly stacked on old wooden tables, my eyes and my hands gravitated toward plush velour and shimmering silk; unfortunately, we were in the market for an insulated nylon shell and a zipper. "Let's pick yellow," Mom said. "That will work whether you have a boy or a girl." My mother was a practical woman and she was confident that a future grandchild of hers would eventually model my creation. When class reconvened and we unfolded our fabric, I was mortified: all the other girls had chosen light blue or pale pink. I knew my yellow parka was going to stand out, and not in a good way, for the whole semester. I tried to apply myself but never finished the anorak. Mom decided to keep it in her armoire: she held on to the belief that I would revisit the project when I became pregnant. She was wrong on both counts.

Marché Saint-Pierre is located at the foot of Montmartre. Largely ignored by tourists who have their eyes set on the Sacré-Coeur, several large department stores (Dreyfus, Reine, Moline) and many specialty shops cater to the rag trade and to private individuals. From dainty lace to luxurious upholstery fabrics, from horn buttons to fancy ribbons, the vast selection draws in stylists, decorators, and hobbyists from all over the country. Meander the path through square Louise-Michel to catch a rooftop view of the Halle Saint-Pierre: the Baltard-style glass and steel structure used to be a covered market and now houses an art gallery and a café. If you're lucky, you may spot the window cleaners rappelling down Dreyfus.

Marché Saint-Pierre
2 rue Charles Nodier, 18th arr.

Bubble

The first movie theater I ever walked into was Le Palace, our *cinéma de quartier* in Vitry. New releases rarely opened on that screen but I loved the whole experience nonetheless: the plush velour seats, the cartoons and the newsreel, the lady usher with her flashlight and her tray of chocolates, caramels, and ice cream... That's where I watched Laurel and Hardy trying to move a piano across a shaky rope bridge in the Alps and Mary Poppins taking flight with her umbrella. Unforgettable. A few years ago, I revisited our old neighborhood but Le Palace had been converted into a sad looking appliance store, another victim of the multiplex mastodon.

On my very first walk through Parc de la Villette, I was specifically looking for La Géode, the giant spherical theater that has played IMAX films for over twenty years. Perhaps I could catch a flick there. But I was having a hard time locating the theater, even with the help of a map. How could I miss a shiny stainless steel ball as tall as a 12-story building? When I finally noticed it, framed between a green edge and the foliage of sycamores, I was stunned: it didn't look like the photographs I had seen. I had been searching for a massive, solid, metallic structure; I found the lightness and transparency of an ethereal soap bubble reflecting the light gray clouds of a cool October sky. A free show; even better than a movie.

Parc de la Villette is the third largest park in Paris, after Bois de Boulogne and Bois de Vincennes. Built in the mid-1980s on the site of the old wholesale meat market of northern Paris, it includes several themed gardens and a large number of cultural venues such as La Cité des Sciences et de l'Industrie, La Philharmonie de Paris, la Cité de la Musique, several theaters and, of course, La Géode. La Grande Halle, a glass and cast iron structure, was used as a slaughterhouse; it's now a venue for art exhibits, fairs, and concerts. Not to be missed: the Garden of the Dragon with its 80 ft slide!

Parc de la Villette
211 avenue Jean Jaurès, 19th arr.

Jules et Jim

We sailed through the whirlwind of life: meeting, losing sight of each other, meeting again twenty-six years later. She had not changed much save for the fabulous silver hair. We reconnected instantly, proof that some friendships do stand the test of time and distance. In a six-hour conversation we caught up on our respective lives; six weeks later we booked a flight to Paris, the city she loves so much. I thought she would enjoy seeing Villa Castel, one of the locations where François Truffaut shot a few scenes of his 1962 film *Jules et Jim*. As luck would have it, a resident timely emerged from the private courtyard and kindly held the iron gate open for us to enter. At the southern end of the cobblestoned alley lined with brick houses, bicycles, and potted plants we discovered a wild patch of greenery: the secluded English garden shown in the film. We could hear boisterous laughter through an open window, along with the clinking of china and glassware: friends wrapping up a leisurely Sunday lunch. I casually chatted with them and I almost felt they would invite us in for a glass of wine. Perhaps we would laugh together like old friends. Perhaps Raegan would imagine herself as carefree as Catherine, Truffaut's heroine in her favorite film, singing *Le Tourbillon*. Her *moment parfait*.

Except for the cimetière du Père-Lachaise, the 20th arrondissement is largely ignored by tourists. Just north of the cemetery, the old neighborhoods of Belleville and Ménilmontant retain the appeal of village life: rue du Transvaal, passage Plantin, rue de Savies, rue des Cascades, villa Georgina, villa du Borrégo, rue Laurence-Savart, villa de l'Hermitage, cité Leroy… these are your destinations to discover pockets of quaint houses and abundant vegetation, the countryside in Paris. Also a must: the panorama from the terrace of the Parc de Belleville, as spectacular as the view from the top of Montmartre, minus the crowds.

Villa Castel
16 rue du Transvaal, 20th arr.

Map